Life By Association: Seeking Slaves

Disclaimer

The people in this book are real and consenting adults that are 18 years of age and older from Rhode Island and the surrounding New England area. However, some information has been altered to protect the identity of the speakers.

The publisher accepts no liability for the content of this book, or for the consequences of any actions taken on the basis of the information provided. You are notified that disclosing, copying, distributing or taking any action in reliance on the contents of this information is strictly prohibited.

By proceeding further than this statement, you agree not to hold the author, publisher or any of the book's sponsors responsible for anything you do, read, write, or think from reading this book. The publisher believes you should be of legal age to read this book, and in the USA that age is 18 years old.

The opinions expressed do not necessarily reflect the beliefs, thoughts or views of the authors or the publisher.

Deliberation and consideration has been used in deciding what to edit and what to leave in this work as a distinctive mark of the speaker's voice.

For more information or to pitch your own story please email JosephS@Santiago-inc.com or balanceheart@hotmail.com

WHAT REALLY MATTERS TO YOU?

***

HAVE A PERSONAL JOURNAL? SUBMIT IT!

***

Examples of submissions are essays, poetry, biographies, creative writings, photographs of your original art, and photographs.

Please go to http://worldvoiceproject.com and click on **Online Submission** to submit your works.

To check out books published under the World Voice theme go to www.Amazon.com and search for World Voice: Speaking Our Truth ISBN: 1937526003.

The NCSF is committed to creating a political, legal and social
environment in the US that advances
equal rights for consenting adults who engage in alternative sexual and
relationship expressions.

We pursue our vision through direct services, education, advocacy,
and outreach in conjunction
with our partners to directly benefit these communities.

https://ncsfreedom.org/

NCSF

822 Guilford Avenue

Box 127

Baltimore, Maryland

21202-3707

(410) 539-4824

ncsfreedom@ncsfreedom.org

Table of Contents

Introduction 8

Seeking Slaves 9

Slave Application 40

    SLAVE SERVICE APPLICATION 41

Continuing On With the Vision for More 84

Hearing from Eli 105

Want to share epic tale with the world? 115

Introduction

This book is the first of a new World Voice series called *"Life By Association"*. In this series we will learn about the diversity of stories and ideas in our world that will inspire us, entertain us, bring people together across physical and cultural borders, and surprise us into the realization that no one thinks and believes exactly as we do. By providing you the reader with the stories that surround us, I hope you can step outside of the box that becomes our lives and discover the world again through another's experiences. Even if we don't agree with the speaker, I believe we all have more in common with each other than we initially realize, and we all have something worth sharing. The story you are about to read started out as a conversation and then became a document that was floated back and forth. I have tried not to edit what is here too much so that the words you read will be exactly as I received it. I hope that the emotions the reader feels will be as interesting and as involved as my own. This story left me questioning many things about relationships and the meaning of love in general.

The stories you are about to read are real and only a few details have been changed to protect the identity of those who sought to share with us the intimacy of their lives. I do not seek to encourage or dissuade anyone by sharing these stories. I merely want the story to speak for itself and give every voice a chance to be heard. I hope you will enjoy having a peek into this *life by association.*

Joseph A Santiago

Seeking Slaves

What you don't know may surprise you…

Joseph: Tell me about you.

Onex2: Are you really interested in me or do you just want me to point out what is different about me and the average person?

Joseph: Answer the question as you take it, but I am interested in the constellation that is you. We are all different and I want to explore those differences with you and what you say will be honored and respected as equally valid choices that are no different than anything I would suggest.

Onex2: Ok. I am in my early thirties and I just graduated from a grad program. I am not quite bisexual. Perhaps hetero- flexible is better, but overall I am straight. I am polyamorous and enjoy love best when it is shared with more than one person. I consider myself a sexual dominant and that doesn't mean I am aggressive all the time, but that I fall into that role naturally when I have sex. Sex is always better when I can feel that I moved someone into their sub-space and I filled myself up with that dominant energy. I am also a very public and private person. I have no problem sharing my opinions and thoughts across a social network but I do not like everyone knowing everything about me. Not only do rumors get spread when a person puts it all out there… they are asking for people to comment and judge. Some people feed off that kind of energy and scrutiny. I don't. No one has the right to demand answers about my personal feelings, life, or intimate thoughts and expect that I will answer them.

JOSEPH: Can we go back a little and would you explain a bit more about sub-space and filling up on dominant energy?

Onex2: Sure. Sub-space is the head space or mindset that a submissive or slave gets into as they feel themselves wrapped up into an experience. There are many different mental triggers that make it happen and it is often more than one trigger that gets someone going into that space. Slapping a girl's ass and making sure she knows you're looking over her body for reaction could start them off. It is not enough by itself and that is the reason we play in many different ways to hit all those sweet spots that make us feel and move. If sticking a cock in and out like a piston was enough every time, and for everyone, then there would be no need for sex games, skimpy outfits, and having a pair of fuzzy handcuffs ready to go for many of us. A sub-space is that interchange of mental and physical stimulation that a submissive or a slave will experience as they get into the head space that transforms that spank into an erotic challenge.

Dominant individuals may describe it as getting into their "dom space", but I have never heard anyone say it that way. I say that I need some dom time, but getting into it feels like taking on the role of a hunter. I feel like I fill up with this energy. I use it to tease, tempt, and fuck. Now that I am saying it, it's more than likely the same thing, but I notice different facets of it, and thus speak of it differently. For a dom getting into that space it's something active. I am constantly reading the reactions of the sub/slave. The activity of the dom is focused outside him and on the scene filled with one or many partners. The sub or slave has an active role also and may be moving all around but much of her focus is on that physical and psychic movement that brings the focus internally. The fit of interaction between the partners will be the biggest factor of how that mental space feels and what kinds of kinks they will explore next.

JOSEPH: Are you saying that everything that is kink is not machine-driven like in and out sex?

Onex2: Yes. There are many rituals that people do not think about on a daily basis surrounding sex. We give flowers to women that we often wish to bed because in Roman and Greek times women would be sent to pick flowers, and it was socially acceptable to spot them, grab them, and fuck them. The woman was then yours and a price may need to be paid to her father. I enjoy consensual non-consent but I would not enjoy or wish to participate in a real rape. I am veering off here. Dressing up provocatively for sex and even dressing as a nurse, school girl, and so much more, are all cultural signals of the ritualized play that we are all taught from a young age. I like a smooth pussy and I like my face freshly shaved or trimmed too. Our life is full of possibilities to imagine and discover a more sensual way to be. The ritualization of multiple elements that we use in our sex lives shares in a global sex culture that very few people talk about. It is constantly fed by movies, music, stories, and our imagination.

JOSEPH: I want to ask you about the distinction you made earlier between sub and slave? If these roles are powerless and without say, how could they be an equal party to a global sexual culture in your opinion?

Onex2: That seems like a loaded question packed with judgments. That is how most people ask questions from their current understanding and world view. I want to point out that your statement either directly or indirectly implies that subs and slaves are powerless and may be victims. While sex crimes do happen and they are terrible, I blame society as a whole for generalizing this to rough play during sex. Religion got it in people's minds that it is somehow better to be violent then to be naked. At the same time most religions have little problem with violence toward oneself and others, repression of anything unapproved in their philosophy, and flagellation of oneself to transcend the everyday experience. I would rather a child see a naked body and people making love than someone being stabbed and tortured to death. The Catholic Church itself has rewritten its own history so that they never mention how they would promote wars so they would be like a festival, and how they would pick the best prostitutes from the brothels that they ran to go out and service the soldiers as they quested for the Grail. To me, the judgment should be on those religions that embraced sexuality and then sought to change how history was told and demonized those people they subjugated only to victimize them later. I am merely talking about the Catholic Church simply because they are who most Americans think of when the term Church comes to mind.

Question your own assumptions. Yesterday's judgments continue on today through many different avenues and are often helped by causes like feminism that are attempting to stay relevant. I agree that women are just as equal to men, but many feminists do not agree that women should be allowed to be happy in a role that they consider less than "female dominant". The cheerleader is one of the more visible examples of this. Cheerleaders compete with each other and cheer at games. There have been many famous feminists that I will not do the honor of mentioning here that have blocked attempts to re-categorize cheerleading as a sport. By changing cheerleading to a sport there would be more funding available for safety gear, spotters to help with training, and better training for accident preparedness. Every year in high school more cheerleaders get hurt than football players overall, and some of those injuries paralyze these girls. Yet because cheerleading is seen as a girly thing to do and feminists do not like women in these roles, they would rather have girls get critically hurt than recognize their right to choose for themselves about what is fulfilling as a woman. It is so much easier to judge and talk about a glass ceiling than it is to recognize when they have gone too far. Getting most feminists to decide what is more important when it comes to this issue usually ends with the feminist stating that *"Women are so much better not going into that role in the first place."*

I believe that feminists who see, who learn about the harm they are causing and do nothing because it acknowledges something they do not wish to promote in their opinion as victimizers. With women like this no wonder universities need Women's Centers on campuses across the world. Feminists are gambling with both boys' and girls' lives in attempt to keep their sexual politics relevant. There are feminist groups that say they want equal rights but seem to be insisting on taking special rights and are more than happy to judge anyone else that does not see all women ready for a powerful role leading the way as worthy.

Submissives and slaves often get stereotyped as being powerless and as victims of another, more powerful person. While this can happen I have seen it happen less than you might think. Many submissive and slaves have good jobs and seek a kind of relationship dynamic that fulfills them. Very few submissives and slaves are in their role all the time and what makes them different is the amount of control they are ready or able to share with their dominate or master.

A submissive may have some hard limits, meaning there are things that they don't want to do or have done to them. A safe word or gesture is also common with a submissive. A slave has given over control about what they should be doing and what may happen to them. That is part of their experience and something that is a constant reminder that they have chosen this way to live. You will hear many slaves who consensually have given their nonconsent speaking of the freedom they have and the experience they have discovered in this role is like nothing else. This idea is threatening to some people because society operates by constantly reinforcing that each of us must be in control at every moment. This is a different way to live but it is as equally valid and important to those people who choose it as the American Dream. I would say it takes more strength of character and control of one's self to allow another to take control than to hold onto the mistaken belief that any of us are in control at every moment.

This global sexual culture is fueled by fantasy, biological desire, and experiential sharing. We all experience our needs and wants differently and having money or other resources certainly helps them get what they want. To the degree they are able to get what they want is how capable they are at contributing to any culture. Today the energy it takes to make an investment in cultural communication is so much easier than it ever has been before. Institutions and agencies used to have a lot of power because they could open up or close off the information that we resonated with, but with the internet and social media, individuals themselves have become more then cultural consumers. We have become generators and producers in such great quantities it has reveled the best libraries of any other point in our recorded history. Individuals have become the producers and generators of cultural content by their stories, purchases, and by sharing what is on their mind with a network group that could be globally reachable with just a tweet. Denying information and culture comes with a risk that it will be gotten elsewhere and the one blocking it off may be transformed into something much less relevant. Every purchase that teases, stings, and pulls a sub or slave around to meet their master makes the global sexual culture even just a bit stronger. I don't think that many people realize that sharing their thoughts can help reinforce or weaken an idea with every open communication and association to it. Even if I reach one person with this message and they reach someone else eventually there is a critical mass that innovates and removes boundaries between people dealing with it. This works for healthy and unhealthy values. What works for me in Rhode Island with an office job and average looks may not work so well for someone else in the exact environment.

JOSEPH: Do you have a sub or a slave presently?

Onex2: I presently have one slave that is mine and there are a few subs and other people that we play with from time to time. Over the years the most I have had is six slaves at one time and I enjoyed working them together.

JOSEPH: Are you a dom or a master?

Onex2: To the girl that I own I consider myself her master. For the subs and slaves that we may play with I would consider myself a dom. The distinction I am making between the two is one of connection, influence, and control. I have those people on loan for the period in which we play. We are not investing in each other's future wellbeing, family, or overall goals. We are often there because we like each other and want to engage in similar activities with good people who are clean, sane, and trustworthy. I recognize the limited time and enjoy it for what it is. I have no problem being called a dom, a master, or even "sir". I have been into Dominance and Submission, or DS, for sixteen years and now that I am approaching 38 years old it is a little funny to be called "sir" by people I am not sleeping with. I guess it is my secret joke from my subconscious mind reminding me not to take myself too serious. Every DS relationship is unique in some way and different people need different things to get them going.

JOSEPH: Can you share a story or a little bit more about how you may interact with your present or past slaves?

Onex2: Good question! Each person has different hot buttons that may or may not be enjoyable pressing at any particular time. I like to begin introducing new scenarios when I have a slave very turned on and they know my attention is on them. I might have a girl blindfolded for the first time and when she is being fucked slowly I may say lean forward so my friend can see your tits bounce. I watch her reaction and I will slowly progress watching her arousal. These are pretty simple examples but as I try out new things I will begin to see what gets her turned on but there is resistance. I push and enjoy what it does to her. I will also pick things she hates simply because I enjoy watching her doing them and enjoy that emotional experience. The slave I have now never had any experience with this role before she met me. She only knew that she had cravings and that the sex she had was not fulfilling enough so I got the pleasure of breaking her in. Today she begs for restraints and to be utilized as a slave. I ensure that any slave that I enjoy knows that the thoughts they think are mine and I will ask for them. I expect they will not hold back and I have them tell me at times, even during an experience, what they are feeling, thinking, and experiencing. If they don't like it I don't have to stop and I may enjoy that they do not like it. Their commitment to obey is what transforms their service into a reality.

It is in the actions of any slave that will wordlessly speak the bold commitment in their intentions to the point that they demonstrate the passion they seek to live by and fulfill the promise of being yours. Their actions speak louder than any words could. Whether I present something she doesn't enjoy, like urine, it doesn't matter to me as much as my pleasure with the responses to these challenges. I enjoy seeing her natural instincts and if I wanted her to respond differently I will say so. I enjoy having my ass licked, and this is called rimming for those who may not know. I like my slave to rim me and I expect her to know how to move her hands across my body in caresses as she does. She did not like rimming me at first and was disgusted with the idea. Seeing how that gradually changed as she felt how it pleased me was a great experience for me, since I do not encourage or require that she must enjoy what I enjoy. She must only be able to perform it to my liking. The enjoyment that comes from recognizing my pleasure is an experience I get to be part of through developing her in her service to me. It is a wonderful experience in itself, and I like making her think about what she is doing and even responding to her thoughts with my own. This creates an intimate connection that is not out of fear but service and love. Does the fact that love can be part of this surprise you?

JOSEPH: I want to be sure we are talking about the same thing. Are you talking about her love for you, your love of what you're molding her into, or a mutual love?

Onex2: Hmmm good question. Can we say that any love between two people is equal and the same? There are many different types of love and having another type of love than your partner does will not make the relationship more or less than anyone else's. Do you agree with that?

JOSEPH: I do agree with all of that. The question still stands about if this is a mutual love or is it something else?

Onex2: This answer will be different for everybody, but for me I do not enter into this kind of commitment where I am responsible for owning another in every interaction we have together, unless I felt I could have love for the slave. That love will be expressed differently for every person and the things that they do will be just as diverse. I seek to create a poly slave house that would have multiple slaves serving me. They would be there taking care of each other and ready to serve the house and me fully. To do this successfully it must be done holistically and it cannot be done without love.

JOSEPH: Would you define poly to ensure myself and those who may read this know exactly what we are talking about?

Onex2: Sure. Poly is an abbreviated form of polyamorous, that means having more than two people in a relationship. "Poly" by itself does not say if someone is married or in a relationship at the moment. It is also a personal identity that lets others know you are open to being in a relationship with more than one person. There are other terms that do describe marriage for poly people. The term polygamy refers to a marriage that has more than one partner and it is the umbrella term for three other forms of poly marriages. To check for understanding now, polygamists are those people that are practicing polygamy in one of the three different forms that fit under this umbrella.

The three forms that fit under the polygamy umbrella are polygyny, polyandry, and group marriage. Polygyny is where one man has more than one wife. Polyandry is where one woman has more than one husband. Group marriage is a marriage that includes multiple husbands and wives. Now I am going to throw a few other terms that are confusing to some people or get thrown into this mix. Bigamy is a crime of marrying one partner while another wife or husband is still living and no valid divorce has been accepted by the Court. The Rhode Island laws are intrusive and will surprise people if they looked it up. I hope this exposure will get the law changed that much faster. *"The act of marrying someone while still married to another is bigamy. Under Rhode Island statutes, a person cannot be married to two persons or cannot live with someone as husband and wife while still married to another person. Bigamy requires a fine of no more than $1,000. A person who commits adultery can be fined up to $500. If a married person has sexual intercourse with someone other than his spouse, he and his partner are subject to the fine."* Read it right from the source at www.rilin.state.ri.us/statutes/title11/11-6/INDEX.HTM and help get the State out of our bedrooms.

Polyamory is the act of having a loving relationship with more than one person which may or may not be a sexually committed relationship. This type of relationship seems to be the most prevalent relationship form for many people today. Polyfidelity is also known by olymonogamy (I do not like this term), poly-committed, and poly-faithful, all mean that three or more people in the relationship only have sex with those in their relationship. It is interesting to note that most religious institutions that believe in polygamy, or more specifically polygyny, are not okay with polyamory, because it is nonhierarchical in nature and both the women and men get equal say. It is the people who seek to take away people's individual rights and believe they have the right to control others without their consent that I think we should be worried about. The problem for many people isn't who is married to who. The problem is some people want to control who can say they are married and that is not okay.

JOSEPH: Can you say more about this slave house you wish to establish?

Onex2: I don't mind if it has a white picket fence... Commitment is what transforms a promise into reality. I am seeking those people who desire to be a slave in a group environment. I want only those individuals who are seeking long term to lifetime commitments. This isn't a joke for me. If people are going to serve me in this capacity they are going to be an intimate part of how I live my life and I theirs. I want people who desire to contribute to the household, and that may mean getting a job and bringing home money. It may mean that they cook and clean, and ensure that the errands get done for the house. Taking on a new slave means they have accepted and they understand that I will lead the way, and they will be ready to fall in line under my direction. These slaves should be semi-optimistic, loyal, and ready to contribute to taking care of house and home. This is a kink family by design.

JOSEPH: What does your current slave think of your plans?

Onex2: She encourages me to find others. She has told me stories of being a child and dreaming of a husband who had another wife to keep him company while she was away. We are a good fit for each other in many ways.

JOSEPH: You mentioned people living in your house. Does this mean you would take on male slaves as well?

Onex2: Yes, it would mean that if I found exceptional males that I found to my liking. I want to make sure my slaves are exercised sexually and having a male is good for that. A woman can certainly strap on one as well, but it is not the same. He would be bound by all the same rules as any other slave, and I would not be against taking on a married couple that are both slaves also. I have talked with a few and have come close already to offering an opportunity to begin my home.

JOSEPH: Do any of these slave couples have children, and if they do how would you work that out?

Onex2: Some of the couples that I have talked to have had children and we both agreed instantly that children would not be a part of this or have any knowledge of it. To them we would be just roommates and upon their 18th birthday there would be a choice to tell them about the life that their parents have chosen. Presently, as you know this is not an issue, and if the house were to work as a family then some things would be able to be carefully hidden from the kids.

JOSEPH: Do you imagine that some of the children would want to join your house on their 18th birthday?

Onex2: I would want to take this on a case by case decision. I value education and believe that even my slaves should be educated. I would want the 18-year-old to go to college and get a degree, and if upon completing a degree program there was still in interest in joining the home as a slave I would more than likely accept them. I have a friend who has two subs and each have children. They live together in Connecticut and have lived as a poly household for about ten years. Everyone works and I believe two of them are taking college classes as well.

JOSEPH: How old is everyone in the house?

Onex2: I'll call him now and you can ask him yourself.

Onex2 takes out his phone and dials. He greets his friend and catches him up on who I am and where we are in the conversation. Onex2 puts the phone on the table and hits the button for speakerphone.

Joe: Hi Joe, I'm Joe too! Onex2 told me he was going to chat with you today and he caught me up on your conversation. All of us are together here and I will put you both on speakerphone so you can ask anything you like. We have about twenty minutes and then we have to go.

JOSEPH: Can you tell me about the hierarchy or structure of your family and relationships?

Jenn: I'll take that question Joe. In day to day life we are all equal and all opinions must be talked out together.

Sue: Hi Joe, that was Jenn and I'm Sue. Nice to meet you. I think we are fairly democratic, though it depends on what the issue may be we are talking about. For instance, sometimes, due to experience, if there is a family situation that needs to be overridden, Joe will, such as if it endangers the family rules.

Joe: Though our relationship includes dominance and submission role play, for the most part outside of the bedroom, it is fairly equanimous.

JOSEPH: How does each person go about solving problems?

Jenn: I assess the situation, and then make a determination of who did wrong.

Sue: I avoid confrontation. And I take in consideration the needs versus wants of the situation. I will try to work things out for myself without others' input.

Joe: We all may ask for input from others, but for the most part if it is an individual decision, we will just tell the others what decision we came to.

JOSEPH: Can you give me an example of a problem that came up, and how it was handled?

Joe: Here's an example that brings unique insights into how I look at the world. Recently, a new relationship energy was brought into our little family. Sue is kinda an addictive personality type, an all-or-nothing individual. At times it is beer, or chocolate, or working out. In this particular case it was new relationships. She went out with one guy on Saturday, one on Sunday and one on Monday. The one Monday stayed for four days straight. Normally this would not bother me. Nor Jenn, however, she forgot to spend time with all of us. The ones in her family. (Only spent about six hours in five days). So we all sat down, and of course at first Sue felt attacked, and scared she would lose us, what girl wouldn't? But then we talked rationally, all of us. And we put everything out on the table. That is what poly is all about, putting your fears out there, knowing all of them will be addressed, and knowing that you are loved. We worked through it, as we have before… Jenn and I made similar mistakes early in our relationships.

In recent months I have been confronted on my drinking. I used to drink *way* too much before Jenn and I got together. And Jenn has been confronted about her overbearing issues with sex. Since then, without the pressures of someone whining about a lack of attention, Jenn says our sex life has improved, along with our cuddle time. And because everyone harped on me, I left the care of a psychiatrist that was detrimental for me. Now I am three months headache free.

These are issues that other guys I work with tell me they could never broach with their wives, or girlfriends. I say bring on the honesty, and the love. I grew up not knowing what jealousy is and still don't. I can honestly say I have never felt that emotion. My parents are similarly poly. We have all the normal issues any relationship has: kids, schedules, work, play, sex. I believe our added dimension is what makes things more honest, we have to be willing to make it work. Finding another guy, or another couple, now *that* has been the true challenge. Poly as a lifestyle is fraught with the preconceived notions that it is not healthy for the kids, or the adults, that love is stretched thin. That is just plain wrong and we are living proof.

JOSEPH: How do you decide what the upbringing of children will be like?

Jenn: (INSTEREO and at the same time) It is a group effort, we answer questions age appropriately.

Sue: (INSTEREO and at the same time) It is a group effort... we are honest and open with the children.

Joe: We raise all the kids as if they are all of ours... as though there are two stepmoms versus one.

JOSEPH: How is work divided inside and outside the home?

Jenn: Outside of the home, we all have jobs. Initially intended for the two women to have part time jobs... somehow we wound up with full time ones. Inside, we all clean and certain tasks are assigned to certain people, but we all help out.

Joe: We all go to school, we all work, and we all raise kids

JOSEPH: How do you decide when to take another mate?

Jenn: -laughter - We get bored with the ones we have... but seriously. There has to be a good fit.

Sue: They have to fit, with everyone, kids and adults. And for the men we have tried to add, not being scared off by the dichotomy of the family.

Joe: Men need to quit being so alpha male. I'm the only alpha male with the women.

JOSEPH: When should or does the marriage include or add others?

Jenn: When everyone is together, and complete and it is time.

Sue: When we have finished adding the people to make the family right.

Joe: In time ... when the times are right, yet we may start marriages before then... yet they would only be for one year and a day.

JOSEPH: What are the values that make this work?

Jenn: Honesty, trust.

Sue: Jealousy has no place here, we will deal with it when it comes up. Flexibility and open-mindedness...

Joe: If it harms none, then do it. The strong protect the weak. And intolerance will not be tolerated. We are all Pagan, maybe that helps? We have to go, but perhaps we can talk again another time.

JOSEPH: I would like that very much.

Onex2: Hope to see you all soon.

How do you imagine it?

JOSEPH: So do you want what Joe has?

Onex2: I like what he has but I want something a bit different. I want a house of people devoted and responsive for my ready command. I want to bring together a house of slaves as its master and leader. The group may have a work life outside the home but their lives are dedicated to growing and developing this house. They will expect to work and serve as they are told. Everyone's skills and gifts will be taken into account so that the house may grow and the quality of our lives will expand with it. Joe has told me before that he wishes there was another guy around that was part of the relationship so that most of the sexual work of the relationship was part of their house routine. There is nothing worse than feeling like the sex you are going to have is just as important as mowing the lawn. (We both laugh at that.)

The males would be able to work together to create more imaginative and fulfilling scenes that they all would enjoy in their dominant and submissive roles. I see the value of having multiple people eager and ready to be of service. Having one or two people fuck your slave with you can be great, but having eight to twelve fuck her silly can be wonderful. What is possible at home and in our sexual play becomes so much more. I crave having that many people responsive to my desire and willingly take on the responsibility. I am not sure how often I would want to go out for a movie with all that right there.

JOSEPH: How many people do you want in your house?

Onex2: I would like to start out with a few and depending on the people perhaps stay at around a dozen. I may go bigger depending upon the house that we are building and the interactions between people. Having an experience like this is something I have found many people dreaming of. I would enjoy shaping and guiding that experience for others. Go out and check out porn. There are many titles with two people fucking because that can be great but there are so many more with three or more people fucking. All of us know there is an instinctive change in desire and intensity when we can be part of something like that. How many actual harems there are today is very likely a very small number, but the fantasy of it lives on and is still a concept that even children read about in books. Society has an unspoken desire to create a family structure so that everyone contributes to one another's welfare.

JOSEPH: How do you plan on finding people?

Onex2: How do most people hope to find a good partner or mate? They put it out there for the world and those in their immediate proximity to find them as they sort through the social cues of individuals that they come into contact with until they find a match for what they seek. To start out I have created a group on FetLife https://fetlife.com/groups/45877 called Rhode Island Crown Court and Harem. The description is as follows.

I have been named King and I seek to establish those people who might serve and please me, as well as those who will help me train the masses. I am seeking those people who wish to begin to offer their service to make this a true fantasy that we can all share. I seek to bring together a core set of people and then have regular real life meetings where the agenda will be set for the future and the serfs and slaves as they toil at their working. The concept here is to combine a harem fantasy with the concept of establishing a Kingdom to make this sustainable. I desire a kingdom and court that will inform and educate, connect people and services, support, and encourage each other, even as you ultimately serve by my whim.

*This is a poly group open to all kinks, sexes, sexual orientations, and loves. The ideal member should recognize they have the desire to serve and be part of something more. This description will be updated as the Kingdom becomes established. I seek to eventually establish a house full of slaves that will recognize my rule. I repeat the **ideal member** should **have the desire** to be part of a harem or kingdom concept because of their **desire to serve** and be **part of something more**.*

I recognize that the description is a little off but I am attempting to explain this and attract people from the larger population surrounding us. It is part of a work in progress. In effect this work and you are becoming my voice that is getting the word out to people I may never have had the opportunity to meet. My profile is _one_x2 on FetLife for those people who already know how good it is to get their kink on. Finally on the digital contact is my email crownhouseone@gmail.com because sometimes it is just easier to reach out and touch someone.

JOSEPH: I am not sure how I feel about the fact you plan on using me as your voice?

Onex2: You wanted to find a real life person who leads an extraordinary life and you did. There is a mutual benefit here that we can both explore as equals. Whomever you choose to explore their life you will be promoting who they are and what they do. What I told you is no different than recognizing and acknowledging that promotion from being included in this work. I am making the best out of the opportunity and don't intend to hold anything back. Are we good?

JOSEPH: We're good and that makes sense. How active is this room you made on FetLife?

Onex2: Presently it is not very active, but that is ok. I want good quality people because they are going to be a part of my life for a very long time. I am happy that the room isn't instantly filling up with people who are not serious or just can't quite make the move to live this right.

JOSEPH: Okay, so what's the next step after you get a hello from someone?

Onex2: This interaction in itself is a helpful one for me as it allows for more refining of my ideas. All that we do after the moment of hello with someone is somewhat patterned on what we have done before. The idea that biography is destiny only goes so far with me. All of us think our behavior makes perfect sense all the time, but try a living experiment. Yes, I realize I am getting slightly off topic but this does relate. When you get with a group of friends that you feel comfortable with, play this mind game. Every time you do something explain your behavior to your friends and don't hold back. Keep a pad with you for all those things that come out of your mouth because the reasons and rationalizations will surprise you.

It is amazing how much emotional and societal baggage we all carry around without realizing it. I call this game *"Behaviorally Why"* and it is one of the things I practice myself to untangle myself from all that is going on that I am a part of so I can honestly begin to examine my associations and meanings I attribute to people and events. Take it too far and it can also be pretty damned annoying. It is a very powerful tool for self-realization and development. Explaining this now may seem out of context, but your questions come preloaded with social constructs of the world and how it should operate. So do my answers by the way... I want to share ways that I have challenged societal expectations and uncovered healthy and unhealthy patterns in my own and other people's behavior because to do better we must choose to learn from that awareness. Please share any reactions you have to this before we go on and I will get to that question now. Okay?

JOSEPH: Sure. Okay. I am more curious now because I am not sure where this will take us next.

Onex2: Back to the question then. It depends on the context that I am meeting someone in. There is the everyday meet and greet, the online hi, and there is being in my role as a Dom meeting someone as they present themselves to me. There are a lot of different ways to go from hello and I am sure you're not interested in the everyday greeting here.

You want to get a sense of transition for different people and how I plan to put this all together. Since most people cannot go outside in full leather or naked but a collar; there are layers of identity, adaptive knowledge of display rules, when to take control, when to release control, and every one of us needs to recognize how to relate together. Being part of any community means you must learn the culture that you are interacting with. For some people they are putting on another hat and do not recognize the world in the same way that they did when they had that other hat on.

Recently I hosted a gang bang of my slave and more than one girl was presented that night. Let me tell you how this night unfolded and you can get a sense of party protocol for how people share their pleasures. My girl shaves her pussy and legs smooth for me and I wanted her to feel sexy for the night's audience. When she is powdered and perfumed she puts her collar on and waits for me in front of the bed. I have her lay on her back and then I cuff her hands and ankles to a spreader bar before attaching that to the bed. Now she can't move and her arms and legs are pushed down against her chest and her pussy and ass is available. This is one of my favorite positions for her. I start to tease her pussy and begin to lightly spank her clit. The spanks move along her thighs and I whip her ass with my hand. I kept the lube in the refrigerator and started to drip it on to her pussy and down onto her anus. All the while she is moaning and begging to show me how good she can be. I will include some photos to bring our play to life.

I take out a six inch glass dildo and stuff it into her pussy. She shivers with the cool glass cock being rocked back and forth. I see how torn she is between the sensation of pleasure and the cool hard cock as she squirms. I move around the bed and put my cock in front of her face and her mouth instantly responds by taking me in. I have trained my girl to suck cock very, very well. She is one of the few girls that I did not train by having her sucking on my cock like a pacifier as I go to sleep at night. She gets so aroused that often I can't help but become more active and I usually end up fucking her. That makes play longer right before bed, but that's another story. She is sucking me and I kneel on the bed and start playing with her ass. Sliding a finger in and out and I see her getting unsure about what is going to happen next. That feeling in her is something I enjoy. I want her surprised and unsure how she got fucked so good. It keeps things fresh.

I push another finger in her and I can see it is a little uncomfortable so I push to one side and then another. I want to slowly stretch her a little before I bring out the next surprise. I get up from the bed and get the new glass butt plug out of the refrigerator and drizzle on the cold lube. She sees it coming and her eyes get big and I know she wants to know what it is I have in my hand. I rest that cold butt plug on her anus and push it in. I feel her clench and she takes it. When it is all inside her it reminds me of a joystick on one of those remote controls for a Play Station. And with my thumb I move it in a 360° rotation a few times as I watch her mouth moving as if she is about to speak. All that comes out is "AAaaa". It make me smile thinking back to it even now.

I slap her ass and she makes a little squeak. I get up on the bed and push my slick cock into her. I know that this is warming her up. I am running through my mind what I will do next. Then there is a knock on the door. The guests are here five minutes early. I feel like I just got done stuffing the Thanksgiving turkey and never got that hot toddy I was thinking about to indulge in a job well done. Guests are here so that mental moment could wait and I was going to enjoy this. I pulled out of my girl and popped the glass dildo back in and told her to "hold onto this". I let three guys into the room and watched their eyes move across my girl. Told them to make themselves at home and put their clothes down in a corner before they came to play. My rule was condoms are a must with all penis contact so expect to put one on before any blow job. "If you want to fuck her ass please do, just make sure you grab another condom for your cock before you insert it anywhere else".

I always like to make sure we have plenty of condoms because I brought a few double headed dildos that were about a foot long. I made sure to place them clearly in sight. They rested right next to different cuffs and restraints to keep it interesting and unsure about what we might do next. It excites me to see that look in her eye where she is excited about whatever comes next. Anyway, they come in and one guy strips and slips a condom on as he starts tea bagging her face. She starts licking his balls and I push back in her pussy hard. The other guy comes up behind me and sticks his hand between my legs to get at the butt plug. He starts playing with it and Eli begins to moan. When that girl is passionately sucking and moaning all kinds of energy resonate through my dick and I know how hard it is to resist her milking the cum right out of you. That is the way I trained her and she has a natural talent with the cock.

We are all playing with her and fucking and she starts to cum. Her body ripples even restrained and she bucks and her whole being works to keep you pumping and inside her. The guy being blown loses it. He can't contain himself anymore and he blows his load. He is shocked and thrilled. I move to reposition her and remove the restraint because I want her to work for every orgasm. This is one of the few times she is allowed to cum freely. This guy gets up and washes himself up and just keeps talking about how good of a cocksucker Eli is. Another guy wants to try her out and the second guy and I take her ass and pussy. I pop the butt plug out and she wiggles a bit with the sensation. I know her ass is still nice and lubed and we all just push in. I spank her ass and watch her squirm happily stimulated. We are all pounding away and I just leave my cock stiffly in place as the guy underneath me rocks in and out. I spank her ass and take her hair in my hand. I'm griping it like I am about to steer a horse in a rodeo. I slap her ass and say, "Show our friends how you cum like a good girl. Cum for me bitch." And she begins to buck like she is a mechanical bull as her nostrils flair with those deep orgasmic breaths. I taught my girl to cum on command and that is something that many people want to see and experience. There is no better experience then to be inside her when it happens.

Now everyone is excited and stimulated to fuck her and make her cum that hard on command. I pop out of her ass and wash up in the sink. As I do, I encourage the three guys to play. I watch them fuck her and fuck her trying to make her cum. She is stuck right there on the edge of cumming and has been trained to cum on command and can cum freely once given the command. I hear the guys tell her to cum like a good girl, but she can't and they all keep pounding her like a greedy slut. She is not allowed to tell them that I am the only voice that triggers these orgasmic sensations and triggers. It has taken me a long time to get her where she is today and it is good to have a student who demonstrates your best work so well. I tell them that "Yes, she can and will cum on command. In fact every time she hears me say the word cum or orgasm that pussy tingles and begins to be stimulated with warm sensations. It is a wonderful tease that drives her wild". The guys don't believe it so they fuck and spank and I see her pussy get pink and her nipples sway and she is vibrating with sexual tension. The guys are getting tired after five minutes of this and I move in closer to her ear. I see her eyes watching me and the hairs on her skin begin to stand up as she gets goose bumps. Her whole body senses me close and is anticipating me speaking these words. "Cum like a good girl." I spank her ass hard. "Cum freely and work for it."

As soon as the words escape my lips Eli explodes with an orgasm that wets the two guys pumping back into her. When my girl gets full of this sexual energy and I allow her to cum, I like to see it explode like a fountain. I can then keep her so turned on that the orgasm sensations doesn't go away and I can preserve that orgasm rolling through her. This time I have been nice. There is another knock at the door and a guy and two girls are there with big smiles on their faces. The door is opened wide and these barely clothed newcomers can see everything that is happening on the bed. I invite them in giving them the same instructions as the other men, but this time I let the two ladies know there are dental dams in the large bag that has the condoms. I have always found it interesting that most women do not bother with dental dams and will just dive in. That thought can be saved for another time.

The men on the bed who are fucking my girl begin to visibly slow as they watch the new girls walk into the room. Both have no panties on with short, short dresses and high leather boots with heels. My friend tells them undress and they smile as they do a wave like motion and they are completely naked except for their boots. The male sits in the chair and pulls down one girl to sit on his cock. The girl squeaks a little and I am not sure if he is in her ass or pussy. At this moment it doesn't matter. He points at the other girl and says, "Down on your hands and knees and lick her pussy." She crawls over a step or two and begin lapping and licking as the other girl works his cock. The male takes her arms and holds them behind the women's back so that she must use her legs to move her and up and down. I like to see a slave's legs grow tired and give out from fucking. It ensures they feel that they have been fucked well and helps to keep them tight and in shape. As I watch the girl licking and the other one pumping, my friend says help yourself. I stick my thumb into the lapping slave's anus and delight in her nervous and excited push back onto it. That instinct is not something that usually comes naturally, and I recognize this as a sign that this is a responsive and well trained slave I am about to fuck.

I reach for a condom and the man says, "I trust you and she is clean. I share her unprotected with very few people. You enjoy, as I am going to enjoy how that slut stays aware of the cum dripping out of her ass for the rest of the night. We are going to the club after this." I took him up on his offer and stuffed a dildo in her cunt. I watched the girl bucking and moaning as she exercised his cock. Both girls were getting turned on and everyone was watching each other in the room. I was rock hard and removed the dildo from her pussy and stuffed it in her ass very quickly. I saw her stiffen and I plunged into that tensed cunt. Grabbing her hair I pulled her head back and moved her face around. I know I would never make a good submissive or a slave. I get hard and ready to play when I am directing the scene. Feeling a slave respond to me, my direction, my desire, my wants, gets me going and tells me that training and fucking good slaves is right for me.

I am free associating with these stories so that we can touch on as many things as possible. Back to the story. I pull out of her pussy and remove the dildo from her ass. She relaxes for a moment as I let go of her hair and her holes are empty. I put the dildo on the desk and begin to spank her ass. One, twice, three times, and she is moving toward me. "Good girl." Comes out of my mouth automatically now… Still smile at the thought of this happening by reflex now. I put the lube on my cock and push inside her. As soon as she feels me enter her ass this girl is rocking and grunting. "My compliments on this one." I say to the man as we both watch the fuck toy on his lap moving and her face is growing red as she sweats. From my left I hear a man moan and he smacks my girl's ass. Then another and I explode grabbing this slave's ass cheek hard and saying, "Cum like a good slut." My girl explodes again and then the two in front of me explode. Right then there is another knock at the door. I move to the door wiping my cock and see a smiling woman with a strap-on.

I welcome her in and quickly say use a condom on your toy and use kinky common sense. "I'm just gonna jump in." she says and the men get up and the girls now move onto the bed to put a show on for us.

I get out another two strap-ons and begin to put condoms on them. "I want you to start fucking my slave." She will be tired and sore by the end of this night and I want her to remember how good she can fuck as I have her sucking me and sore later. The girls take them from the side of the bed and now there are three strap-ons in play and each girl starts to mount Eli. I put a few condoms and a trash can on the side of the bed so they can quickly switch holes and take turns at every position. The girls circle and pump relentlessly and after half an hour of doing this one of them asks for a drink. They all take a water bottle and drink as the men start to circle them and we pick a hole and fuck it. This whole play party lasted 3 hours and we worked up an appetite. I put the glass butt plug back in Eli and then half of us went out to a dinner.

I loved squeezing her ass knowing that the sensations would still be stimulating her. I smiled on as we chatted and she spoke confidently and cheerfully about the party and the day over dinner. It takes a good girl to focus on what is happening with a vibrating butt plug stimulating from deep within her ass.

Slave Application

Onex2: So you can tell that context and relationships mean a lot to us as we live and play together. I am not sure I answered your question.

JOSEPH: Sort of but not fully. You did share an interesting story that demonstrates not only circumstances but how you and others think about subs and slaves.

Onex2: Doms, domes, masters, mistresses, and many more titles that are intended to communicate dominance or the opportunity to share service will require a sub or slave to fill out an application for service. I will share a simple application for that here. You can find a practically unlimited supply of different versions of this by searching on the internet for "Slave Application". I want you to imagine having to fill one of these out. It is not always as simple as having the desire to serve and then you go out and become an expert fuck slave. You have to be chosen and you must be able to demonstrate that you have thought about this realistically to some degree. We want to make sure we have kinky, capable, and psychologically healthy people. This is also a bit of a background check and the sub/slave must get used to the idea that the impression they make represents the owner, master, etc., and their history is there to be inspected and called into question.

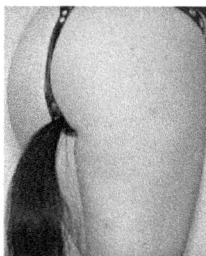

SLAVE SERVICE APPLICATION

Application to be held by: _____-___

Date inquiry was received: /   /   /

Date Application was sent: /   /   /

Date of Receipt of completed Text: /   /   /

First name and initial:_____

Slave Alias: _____

Current Mailing Address:

_____

City:_____

Zip Code:_____

Specify:

Home Or Business Phone #: (   )   -

Email address:

Chat names and service used:

THIS IS YOUR APPLICATION REGARDING CONSIDERATION

FOR THE STATUS OF;

"SLAVE"

I AM A Master. This is your application regarding
"CONSIDERATION FOR THE STATUS OF SLAVE." I expect this
questionnaire filled out fully and completely. Failure to answer ANY
question, or heading will result in automatic FAILURE. YES, this is a
test. LIES OR PART TRUTHS demonstrate you are not ready for an
intense relationship where you recognize your thoughts and actions
belong to a Master. If you are accepted as mine you should know that
anything YOU DO reflects on me and our relationship.

This information will not be posted online or shared in a public way at
any time. This is your first test of trust and our bond begins with
showing me you have that trust now. Filling in this form will take

time. A good Master needs a thorough understanding of any slave who is accepted under his control, and honesty and trust are established through clear communication, as well as good actions and training. The mental component to slavery is just as important as the physical dimensions, and this application will help a slave to begin to explore the mental side of slavery so that we ensure there is a mutual understanding.

Your pictures: Insert body, face, and profile pictures here.

Height :   Weight :

Date of Birth :   Age :

Hair Color :   Eye Color :

Ethnicity :   Nationality :   Citizenship Status:

Professional status :   Marital Status :

Driving License? Yes or No   Sexual Orientation :

HIV Status :   Last tested for health STDs: Live Alone? :

Able to accommodate :   Able to travel :

Smoke: Which brand and how many? :

Drink alcohol: What type of alcohol and frequency?

Take Drugs? What type of drugs and frequency?

Body Shape: Overall Looks:

Cock Diameter - flaccid	Cock Length - flaccid
Cock Diameter - hard	Cock Length - hard
Cut/Uncut	Testicles (S/M/L)
Waist Size	Leg Length
Chest Size	Collar Size
Shoe size	Head Hair
Facial Hair	Body Hair

Have you ever been loaned out sexually or for service?

What are your thoughts on this being loaned out?

Have you had threesomes or group sessions?

What are your thoughts on these experiences?

What has been the longest relationship you have ever had and what type of relationship was it?

Are you able to be faithful?

Do you currently have any master-slave relationships, or regular partners? If yes describe them completely.

Do you currently have any vanilla relationships, or regular partners? If yes describe them completely.

Which do you consider yourself to be?

Exclusively top or dominate

Equally top and bottom (level switch)

Usually top, occasionally bottom (top heavy switch)

Usually bottom, occasionally top (bottom heavy switch)

Exclusively bottom or slave

Other: Describe using this scale your present service identity

If you switch roles, which role do you feel most comfortable in?

Do you consider your current interest in slavery or sexual service to be light, moderate or heavy? Give two or three examples.

Do you consider your experience of slavery or sexual service to be novice, intermediate or experienced?

Describe your first sexual experience.

Describe your first master-slave or sexual service experience.

When was your last master-slave relationship and how long did it last? (Describe it)

List any leather, uniform, rubber, or other clothing items you own.

List any toys, tools, or equipment you own.

Do you have access to or frequent a playroom or dungeon? (Describe if yes)

Do you have any medical or physical conditions which may affect your ability to be slave? (Explain)

List any dietary dislikes, allergies and preferences.

Read and contemplate the following quotes. Then, write your responses to the questions which follow, ensuring your responses are on the line beneath each question, aligned with the bullet point above and are in bold font. Answers must be written honestly, indicating what you currently believe, and not what you assume to be my beliefs or desires.

<u>Committing to a term of slavery (lifetime, long term, specified term of service) is a solemn commitment for anyone to consider.</u>

What is commitment?

What would you find difficult about commitment?

What would prevent you from committing totally to a master?

What are the implications of committing to this sort of lifestyle permanently?

The rules and set conditions are designed to be built up over time and have no fundamental meaning onto itself. Rituals and protocol are a means to an end and represent the culture and connection of the relationship. Each slave may have a slightly different protocol or ritual that is sustainable, always maturing and evolving around a connection between a master and slave partnership.

Are you prepared to live a life governed by rules and conditions?

What if you do not agree to some of the rules and conditions set by your master?

Are you prepared to be used and trained to obey these rules and conditions, even if you do not agree with them?

How would you cope with the rules and conditions changing over time, as you mature in your service?

How would you envision a natural progression of your service would be like as my slave?

How can you, as the slave, ensure the relationship is effective and mutually satisfying?

I own your body, mind, and spirit. I expect only for you to be honest, open, and truthful, with yourself and me, your master. Even when that honesty is not easy it is mine to be heard and receive.

How important is honesty? Give examples.

What would prevent you from being honest?

Would you find it difficult being honest about something negative, knowing that you would possibly be punished? And if so, how could this be rectified?

Should a slave keep things from his master? If so, what? If not, why is it important not to keep things from a master?

How would you approach an issue you knew was in conflict with your master?

How difficult has it been for you find honesty in your relationships?

Is being honest on paper, email, and text easier than face to face? Why?

How important is negotiation in a master-slave relationship?

Should a slave have the right to negotiate?

Should a slave merely be told what to do all the time?

Should a slave be like a robot, following all orders blindly and without question from his master?

Should a slave have the right to establish boundaries?

What if these boundaries conflict with something a master wants to explore?

In this sort of relationship, are both roles representing an equal partnership of sorts, at least while the negotiations are taking place?

Does a slave have any rights to dictate how the relationship is going to progress?

Can a slave demand that boundaries are fixed and immutable?

Can a slave change his mind about boundaries and other things he or she has negotiated on?

<u>Some slaves come into the lifestyle expecting everything to be like they fantasized about it and perfect.</u>

What is your idea of a perfect relationship?

What qualities do you bring with you to support a relationship?

What would hinder you from establishing a perfect master-slave relationship?

What difficulties would have to be faced and overcome to grow through a master and slave commitment?

Is a perfect relationship attainable at all?

How do you recognize that your master-slave relationship as mutually beneficial?

What turns you off or you simply have come to accept about slavery?

Do you have any special dreams or fantasy situations you'd like to try?

What are your qualifications and skills that will be your successful foundation for your slavery?

Do you wish to be in this type relationship 24/7 or only during specific scenes?

24/7, only during scenes, only at specific times? If your role can be turned on and off how would you describe the cues in the environment that could be set so that you could signal you wanted the master-slave aspect of the relationship to start and stop?

Is a part-time slave still a slave?

Should slavery be defined by the time spent in slavery?

What are the benefits or drawbacks to these different types of relationship while they use these labels?

Are you seeking, in time, to become a live-in 24/7, permanent slave, living the lifestyle completely?

Are you prepared to give up preferences and act as directed in performance of your service? This will apply to more than the music you listen to and the TV you might be allowed to watch.

Should a slave be allowed to contribute ideas to the relationship?

Is it reasonable for a master to deny a slave choices of music, books, film etc?

Should a slave be directed to listen to specific types of music, read specific books without due regard to the slave's opinions, likes and dislikes?

How easy and ready should a slave be to deny his own likes in favor of his or her master's?

Should a slave be made to give up his or her own likes if the master requests this?

When should a master use rewards, punishments, and discipline to implement a decisions on these matters?

Being tired, ill or being in a bad mood does not excuse you from your required tasks. Communication about your duties and any illness would not be optional.

Is it reasonable to expect a slave to be a slave when he or she is ill, tired or feeling off?

How strict should a master be in enforcing what he or she requires of a slave?

Should a slave have the right to say no to their master?

How would you cope with being told to do something you were not in the mood to do, scared to do, or disgusted by?

How difficult and how beneficial would doing more than you were comfortable with in the moment create a stronger person from the commitment to your slavery?

Does a slave have the right to question his or her master?

Individuals can choose to enter a commitment of service as a slave. Those who enter into this life consensually are making a valid relationship choice that offers mutually beneficial opportunities to live a life that matters to them and others. The choice to live as a slave can also allow that person to know utter freedom.

How much freedom should a slave have when in the relationship?

Should a person be forced into slavery?

Do you think you would require the threat of punishment to carry out your slave duties regularly and well?

Does a slave have choice in his or her slavery, or does the slave merely obey?

Are force and threats necessary? Is it desirable? Some slaves crave to be forced to obey. What are your thoughts on this matter?

Is free will important for a slave?

How much freedom would you, as a slave, require? And in which areas?

If I as your master tell you that can't do something, you simply can't do it.

How difficult, or easy, would you find this statement when it is testing yourself control and impulsivity?

How is your temper? How do you become angry?

Would you find a strict or a loose master more difficult to obey and why?

Would you seek ways of rebelling or be passive aggressive?

In which areas and in what ways have you rebelled in the past?

How do you think a master should deal with a rebellious slave?

Anyone who seeks to be honestly recognized as a slave must enter into the life with their eyes wide open, and knowing that what they get is not always what they could have planned or guessed.

What are the most important things you are expecting to get from a master-slave relationship?

What do you expect to be easy?

What do you expect to be difficult?

How sincere are you about slavery?

Ultimately, how important is slavery and your service to you?

Are you prepared to work hard at developing yourself through your service to me?

Is the idea of slavery a passing whim in your journey through life?

How permanent do you want your slavery to be?

Being a slave means giving up all attachments except those that bind you to your service. This is much different than simply being only a submissive. All that you are belongs to me and you become my everything. All that you are is given over to me. Slavery must be more than a mere word. It's a defined action, a way of life, and a lifestyle that connects one heart, mind, and spirit completely to the owner(s). You will become a true artisan of service.

Are you prepared to give up all rights? Is this a reasonable request at this moment?

Are you prepared for slavery as a way of life?

Understanding that slavery is service what would be your short and long term relationship goals?

Would being owned provide you with what you have been looking for in life?

Have you ever sought to be owned before?

This next section deals with your past and present preferences, experiences, and knowledge of BDSM activities. Just because it is listed here does not mean I am into this. The following scale should be used while reading this list over. Put the corresponding number next to the activity listed.

0 - NOT INTERESTED

1 - BARELY INTERESTED

2 - SOMEWHAT INTERESTED

3 - INTERESTED

4 - VERY INTERESTED

5 - EXTREMELY INTERESTED

Humiliation

Body worship (kissing)

Body worship (licking)

Body worship (massage)

Boot kissing

Boot licking

Butler duties

Chauffeur duties

Chef duties

Crawling

Dirt

Dirty words

Eye contact restrictions

Food on body

Forced exercise

Forced nudity (around others)

Forced nudity (private)

Forced nudity (public)

Forced servitude (domestic)

Furniture use restriction

Human ashtray

Infantilism

Kneeling

Lead by collar

Mud

Physical humiliation

Public display

Public embarrassment

Spit

Stand in corner

Valet duties

Verbal abuse

Verbal humiliation

Forced Feminization

Writing on body (permanent ink)

Writing on body (washable ink)

Ass play

Beating (hands only)

Belt

Biting

Blood

Canes

Cat o'nine tails

Cutting

Face slapping

Flogging

Genital Control

Handcuffs

Hand spanking

Harsh marks

Heavy bruising

Kicking

Leather paddle

Made to cry

Mild bruising

Mild marks

Mild torture

Moderate beating

Moderate bruising

Moderate marks

Needles

Over the knee spanking

Permanent markings

Pegs (body)

Piercings

Pinching

Punching

Pushed to the limit

Rattan cane

Riding crop

Rubber whip

Soft beating

Tattoo

Wax

Wooden paddle

Arms restrained

Bondage - Being stretched (face down)

Bondage - Being stretched (on floor)

Bondage - Being stretched (on rack)

Bondage - Being strung up (not touching floor)

Bondage - Being strung up (touching floor)

Blindfold

Boxed

Cage

Chains

Cling film

Cock and ball bondage

Cock rings

Cock straps

Duct tape bondage

Full body rope bondage

Full head hood

Gagged

Gas mask

Immobilization

Isolation

Kidnap

Legs restrained

Sensory depravation

Manacles & irons

Mental bondage

Mind control

Mind fucking

Mummification (complete body)

Mummification (partial)

Partial head hood

Rope

Rotating X-shaped cross

Short time periods

Wrist and ankle cuffs (leather)

Wrist and ankle cuffs (metal)

X-shaped cross

Electro play

Anal Play

Anal inspection

Anus stretchers

Bareback fucking

Butt plug at home

Butt plug in public

Chilled objects

Extra large butt plug

Extra large dildo

Fantasy rape

Fisting

Food as dildo

Food on body

Frozen objects

Fucking strangers

Large butt plug

Large dildo

Large vibrator

Medium butt plug

Medium dildo

Medium vibrator

Metal

Milking

Mouth fucking

No lube

Prostrate massage

Rimming clean ass

Rimming mod. clean ass

Rimming dirty ass

Rough fucking

Sling

Small butt plug

Small dildo

Small vibrator

Speculum

Forced to fuck

Warm objects

Wear panties

Drink cold piss

Drink piss from cock

Drink piss from bowl

Piss bed

Piss control

Piss enema

Piss fuck

Piss gags

Piss ice-cubes

Piss in clothing

Piss in drinks

Piss in food

Piss in mouth (not swallow)

Piss in mouth (swallow)

Piss in ass

Piss on body (including face)

Piss on body (not face)

Public piss

Public piss in clothing

Wash in piss

Wear pissed-in underwear

Behavior rules

Breath control

Cyber control

Hair removal

Hypnosis

Master chooses clothes

Master chooses food

Phone control

Rituals

Sexual deprivation (long term)

Sexual deprivation (short term)

Sleep deprivation

Clean shitty ass (with hand)

Clean shitty ass (with paper)

Clean shitty ass (with tongue)

Eat shit

Eat shit cooked in food

Enema (hot)

Enema (warm)

Enema (cool)

Enema (chilled)

Enema (cleansing)

Lick cock while master shits

Shit control

Shit fuck

Shit in bucket

Shit in clothes

Shit in confined space

Shit on body

Dog Training

Barking

Drinking from bowl

Eat from bowl

Eat from floor

Fed from hand

Feltch in mouth

Growling

Howling

Lead

Outdoor piss

Outdoor shit

Suck toes

Massage

Fucked by feet

Orgasm control

Tickling

This is by no means an exhaustive list of kinks and distractions to engage in with slaves. I do want to mention the slave registration number website. This website provides a central place for the registration of slaves and submissives. Each registration is assigned a unique Slave Registration Number ("SLRN"), and owned submissives and slaves can display an ownership certificate. Right at this moment 154858 slave registration numbers have been issued. www.slaveregister.com It is a great idea and I wish I had thought of it first. I also recommend you check out The Eulenspiegel Society http://www.tes.org and The National Coalition for Sexual Freedom https://ncsfreedom.org/ as they are excellent sites that provide information for both the novice and the wise in our community.

JOSEPH: Do you have Eli on there?

Onex2: No, I never asked her to complete a profile and since I developed her as a slave she may never have even seen this site. The site is a warm fuzzy for kinky people who want some sort of certification that they have a slave in their home stable. We all do what we do for different reasons and I am not someone who concerns myself with how other people are buttering their toast when everyone is happy.

Continuing On With the Vision for More

JOSEPH: Now that you have shared a bit more, I am curious, how is it you imagine discovering all these people who want to build this slave house with you?

Onex2: One of the most likely places is online where people may stumble across our profile, posts, or start to interact with Eli or myself in a chat room. There we have the ability to ask many of these questions that are in the slave application and discover how optimistic or pessimistic a person is in life. Attitude is important because some people depend on others to motivate them or their mood to change. Finding that right combination of personality and physical traits is not as easy as ordering off the menu, and even when I have thought there was a fit something can prove itself to be off. It could be that someone has too much baggage or supervision. It could be that they have finical problems that follow them. There is no limit to the problems a person can bring or discover.

I think half of the people we will find online and the other half will be from introductions and contact within the kinky world. I don't make the mistaken belief that everyone fits into neat boxes or that they will often think like me. Having a tool like an application for those face to face interactions allows me to begin to ask questions that bring the different parts of our experiences, tastes, and wants to be contrasted in relation to one another. It also brings up many interpretations that start conversations that will uncover if there is a problem and help me determine if this is a person I want to be with and who will represent me in social circles. There are two circles that we all represent ourselves and our identities every day. The first social circle is the proxemic circle, which are those people that we meet up with face-to-face. The second circle is the network circle, and this group is comprised of the people we interact with through our many social networks. There is often a lot of overlap between these two circles.

Creating distinctions about these circles allows us to plan interactions for people entering and exiting them. If I am inviting someone to become part of my day to day intimate life there is going to be a screening process. There will probably be a trial period of consideration and there will be a lot of communication about how they will fit and what our interactions will be like. Guess what! This is the same process that any other personal or professional relationship would have to go through.

A distinction I have is that one or more house slaves that could be male or female, can exclusively contribute to the house and only be enjoyed now and then as sexual extras. This person could be like a butler and they would be the perfect house help. They may work outside the home to bring in money and work inside the house to contribute and offer their service. I want something sustainable and that means taking the time and the effort to find people that want to put in the work to experience the joy of their commitment and service. This is not for everyone and people should be picky about where their time is spent. For this reason I believe that some roles can be developed for the good of all.

JOSEPH: It sounds like there may be a few different versions of how to best accomplish this. Is that right?

Onex2: All major projects and goals must be accounted for and be ready to adapt and change. It is best to plan for it and design it into the model so that as the pieces start coming together they can be managed strategically. I plan on developing a philosophy for the house that will extend to all the things that we do. There will be common rules and guidelines so that everyone will be able to know and recognize when someone is working successfully for the house and when they're not. This is simple group dynamics at work. Individuals will have certain behavioral traits but when people come together as a group the behaviors that individuals may express can be outside of what they would have sought to do on their own.

JOSEPH: Have people ever told you that this design may resemble a cult?

Onex2: Most organizations and competitive companies operate with a mission statement, philosophy, strategic plans, and loyal followers that seek out that brand because it is good. I do not want to isolate people from the everyday world. I want people to be part of something more and satisfy their desires to contribute to those who will appreciate it and them. I am talking about establishing relationships that define and enhance the way we live our lives. I do not seek to take advantage of anyone and those people who may see it that way are attempting to frame life as a transaction. I am talking about creating an alternative family form and doing it in a way that satisfies the needs and desires of the people who choose to be there. There is a big difference here.

JOSEPH: How will you manage disagreements or people wanting to leave?

Onex2: First, I would be open to having a contract that sets a time and date to be driven to the airport, train station, or coffee shop, to go back to another life. Otherwise this would be similar to what you would have to do when you shared a place with a roommate or a sibling. No one always wins and at times a higher authority may come in to decide things for you that make you both unhappy. No one ever will be forced to stay there and it doesn't make sense to look for people that want to immediately leave. There must be a trust that extends to everyone because we will all be cooking and eating food that will be shared. We all will be sharing spaces that will give everyone opportunity to know where we each need help or support. Everyone will be different in where they are mentally, physically, spiritually, and emotionally. Doing this together is starting an adventure that once tasted it will never be forgotten.

JOSEPH: Do you expect people to believe you're setting up a slave household to better other people's lives and you're not getting anything out of this?

Onex2: These would be collared slaves, and I know that means different things to different people, but people outside of this life should not think their label for a relationship is any better than mine. Giving a collar to someone is extending a commitment about the seriousness of the relationship between you. In every relationship there is give and take and somebody may carry a bigger load. If the relationship is a healthy one all partners will seek what seems to them to be a balance. That balance may look different in a MS (master slave) relationship but so do a lot of marriages and friendships. Every person who is part of my house will get something meaningful out of it and will contribute to the welfare of all who go there. I find an exceptional amount of meaning and intimacy in the connections I have with my slaves. Every slave may have different arrangements with me about the type of slavery they desire and how other people judge that is not anyone else's concern but ours. We talked before about playing devil's advocate for many of these questions and I recognize that people who know nothing about me or my kink will blurt out many questions. Some of those questions are rude and show a level of ignorance. Your questions do not show ignorance but they do carry with it the discrimination that many of us have encountered in our lives when sharing who we are with others. We have a coming out process that happens every time we meet someone new.

This discrimination is a reflection of society and some people automatically distrust anything that is different than what they have encountered before. If someone goes up to two gay males and asks them which one in your relationship is the girl and who is the guy? That is mocking them with judgment and there is a clear difference between someone who doesn't know and doesn't have the right words. We can tell when people are being a dick. For many of us we pick our battles and we just allow you to be the dick and see if you actually get to know us so the discrimination will fall away. We are part of this society and what is hilarious to me is that people who are judging me don't even seem to be aware of the level of kink and love that surrounds them every day. All they are looking for is sex, gender, love, religion, and so much more, in this one package that they have established for themselves as it.

Years ago there was this song on the radio called "One Thing" by Finger Eleven that ran with this sentiment that everyone had something they were yearning for. The best part about the song was, what the one thing was is never shared. The song allowed the listener to reflect what came into their mind and heart. I would have more than one thing come up at different times when I heard that song, but I was able to still relate to the singular idea that one thing could be something that we all were yearning for expression. When asking good or bad questions, ask things to be defined and don't think any one of us can guess who someone else is. I do not represent all people who are poly. I am not going to pretend there are not bad people out there that would seek to take advantage of others. I am going to say that if people only see good or bad people with these childlike filters of what is good and bad they will become preyed upon more easily. I am still surprised when I allow people to speak freely and I learn much more about the person and the world as they see things. If I was in my head judging everything that came out of someone's mouth I would stop responding to the person in front of me and I would begin listening to the person inside me. It is too easy to do this and going further as I start to think of what will I say before the other person is even done speaking. Doing this is something everyone should expect to feel judged for.

When a person is focused into something, they have to read and understand, and if there is someone sitting next to us talking loudly, we get distracted. We do not take in what is really going on and we miss cues that would allow a person to ask questions to understand better and perhaps create a stronger connection through dialogue. One of the most common complaints I hear from people outside of this lifestyle is they are having trouble connecting meaningfully with others and they desire to feel more from their relationships. It seems to me that they are not making their focus the thoughts, experiences, or adventures, which will get them to enjoy what and how they want to live their life. Restraint is a needed part of discipline, but I believe that many people go way too far with it. I know I can't be the only one who has witnessed someone else's idea of control get out of control. This is from someone who enjoys control but I don't push that control onto other people. There is so much control exerted on us by institutions and society in general, that people seek to just let go in increasingly more personal and profound ways.

JOSEPH: Can you give some examples of how you see people letting go more profoundly?

Onex2: Should I submit this in a 69 word essay? (We both smile and laugh a little) The way we live, and let me just say I am only speaking as a member of the American society, the way many of us live is disassociated from the sensual experiences of living. So we grab bigger TVs to immerse ourselves in stories that have intense experiences. When we step away we keep ourselves level and in check to keep thinking about idle things and chores. Getting into a routine where we are comfortable and we all seek to minimize risk. So much of what we see is sanitized so that it will not offend or remind us that there may be another way to live. Many people in the US have gotten in the habit that food can change the way they feel and so they don't have to move very far or very fast to do much differently. All they have to do is be a consumer and that is a behavior approved of by many societies these days around the globe. So much care is taken for people to just indulge in pleasures and eating should be counted as something beyond a biological need for many people in America. Companies who seek to cater to our food fetish help us with the illusion that food somehow appears as food. Meat is often prepared in ways that disguise the fact that it actually came from a living breathing animal.

There are wonderful pieces of music and today they sell HD radio, satellite radio, streaming music, surround sound speaker systems, noise canceling headphones, devices that can hold well over 10,000 complete albums. Not only do people want to be swimming in experiences, that want to be reminded about it and have it as real as possible. I read as a kid that one issue of the *New York Times* had more information in it than the average person in the early 1800's would have read over their whole life. Look how far we have come, but will we ever know the freedoms we have gained and lost in comparison to even a hundred years ago? Some people will even say that we have physically stopped adapting because we have yet to sprout an eye in the middle of our forehead. Yet we cultivate that information and it changes us, but our animal urges are still very much there as well. More and more, all of us seek to explore experiences and ways of living that feel right to us. Sharing those experiences of living becomes an expression of our individual freedom and that inspires us more.

JOSEPH: It is beginning to sound like you are talking about your kink as being integrated into a philosophy of self-improvement and social change. Am I understanding this correctly?

Onex2: Yes you are. What we call our kink are the things we keep coming back to because we like them a lot! So if we want to share the best of something why shouldn't we share it with the how and the why of how it makes us a better person? Sharing what makes us better often transforms society so that we can understand another person and another way of thinking. Being passionate about something often means we are becoming more knowledgeable and informed about the topic. We seek out all the intersections of knowledge and how it is being put to use. This is no different than loving to hike and then working with the knowledge until you're ready to walk across mountain tops. Many books have been written about hiking and mountain climbing that have demonstrated that being passionate and seeking to master anything will begin to share perspectives and skills that will become useful in other areas.

I would love to be taught by someone who is passionate about a subject and lived their life in a way that exemplified a value of what they wanted to see in the world. It is easy for people to discriminate and treat anyone differently if they don't have a way to process or understand the differences that are presented to them. That is the reason why every one of us seeks to qualify what we reveal to others as we do not wish to be judged or discriminated against. In every society we are taught to recognize the differences, and as we get older, the differences that we notice have many ways that they could be interpreted by society. It is not the person that people are resisting, it is the differences that the person begins to represent and demonstrate. Because of the internet and the free flow of information, the diversity of cultures and the people who come to represent those differences must also think about how to make those differences digestible for others who know nothing about them.

Every one of us must come to see ourselves as furthering information that make it better or worse for people to share who they are with each other and in our communities. We are having an engaging talk about having more than one adult live together in a house because they all may have sex. That becomes even more interesting because we are open and honest about the social dynamics surrounding the way that we choose to live and want to find likeminded people to build a future with. How we do that, and the stories of the people we meet along the way can be funny, disturbing, and informative. Maturing into a perspective that allows you to think that the person you may be talking to might not be heterosexual, they may not want to identify as male or female, they may not want to have the equal control about what happens in their home, they may not want to pretend they can only be in love with one person at a time, they may not want to give up most of what matters to them in their personal lives to be in a career, and they may not want to think and live exactly like you. To some people these are earth shifting statements because they can't imagine what life would be like any other way then how they have been thinking about it and living it. Some of us have wanted it so different from how we are experiencing and living it that these changes can't come fast enough.

By sharing who we are and sharing our stories in many different ways with people around us, we can see that they are beginning to see the humanity within us. That all of us still want many of the same things and that peaceful partnership allows for areas of our lives to be shared so that we all can discover better and healthier ways to live. None of us have the perfect relationship form that is universally guaranteed to give happiness. All of us have things in our life and experiences that aren't easy to talk about, and if what we are sharing here today makes it a little easier for someone else to talk about what they are feeling or going through, then I am happy. People are bullied because they are different and they are discriminated against by others who want them to be something different than they are. If we find the words we can make it easier for that not to happen and seek help to make sure people do not have to go through these intentionally isolating experiences alone. When someone wants to force a choice on you they will attempt to cut off any other choice than those choices that are acceptable to them. This is an influence attempt to make you conform and there are times where this may be appropriate and there are times when it is not. Part of being able to share what is going on with others becomes part of the learning that will help us all to determine if an influence attempt that is forceful is good or bad. One person can make a difference in the world and that starts by inspiring and communicating with the people right in front of us.

JOSEPH: Does the influence attempts to society mean as much because you're not attaching your name to it?

Onex2: Would the ideas of Gandhi, Martin Luther King Jr., Tony Robbins, Dan Millman, Richard Bandler, Alfred Nobel, Albert Einstein, Oprah, and so many more, have any less of an impact because the name they used was not their own? It is the package that the ideas come in I hope will be meaningful to others. The names you see above do not do justice to the accurate information of their lives. We know nothing about their struggle, the challenges they overcame, and the stories that we do know have taken on a mythic dimension.

These people have become a philosophy that is a kind of brand onto themselves. Companies like Apple know this and have produced innovative products around a cult-like reputation that deals with information in the same way as any religious institution. Companies and religious institutions have more in common than most people realize. These institutions create messages and products that are meant to entertain and define the way we think about much of the world and ourselves. All of us have varying levels of self-acceptance about ourselves and with different aspects of our identities. I think it is a terrible thought crime to allow another person to blindly accept stereotypical limitations with the intent of marked segregation. I believe reframing the idea of discrimination as a problem of cultures clashing will allow individuals to more easily become aware of areas in their own life where they can have some control. Just as there are plenty of examples in the world that depict negativity and pain, there are just as many that demonstrate the strength of those people who were not satisfied with hearing "no". Those people are the models that can point the way to undiscovered territory for us all. To find what is undiscovered, a person must start by looking within themselves to ask the question of what it is that they want for themselves in this life. I am taking this opportunity to do that here and hoping to inspire those who read this to do the same.

JOSEPH: You think that by sharing openly who we are people will experience the benefits, or will it create more drama?

Onex2: If a person wants to create drama they can choose anything no matter how simple or complex. Think back to when you were in high school and imagine there is a fight going on and there are twenty people all circled around the opponents yelling at each other and taking swings. Are the people surrounding the fights creating drama?

JOSEPH: No they aren't, but they are also not directly participating.

Onex2: A person on the sidelines never encourages or discourages people to fight?

JOSEPH: Of course they do. People could also break up that fight and get people past the aggression or make it worse.

Onex2: So drama is not the problem. The lack of communication and understanding has helped to support a set of circumstances where people feel at odds with each other. At any time people can interrupt this and bring in additional information and make people aware of consequences for their behavior. All of us have to create inroads to more peaceful ways so we can change minds without making people feel like they are losing face or being proven wrong for recognizing another valid perspective.

While individuals must communicate with each other in daily life, we all must make inferences (whether right or wrong) about the attitudes and attributes from the people and groups that surround us. By allowing people the space to express who they are, we will discover a lot of things in our interpersonal relationships that we didn't know before and may never have guessed. The first thing that must be clarified is our own individual values so that we can ask the person or people we are talking to about theirs. Our conversations now seek to explore what they are feeling, experiencing, and would like out of any interaction. Showing a genuine desire to learn and know more about a person who is talking to you is not something I have ever experienced many people wanting to resist. Clarifying our own ideas and values on a topic gives us a clear mind that can compare the ideas and position on a matter. People do not have to leave agreeing, but they will both be able to voice what their goals are and inquire about the different possible meanings and perspectives that would create an opportunity to get where they want to be. Now there is little to no resistance for the person bringing the difference into the conversation. The information talked over is taken back with all parties even when they leave each other's company. Sharing sex should be a transformative experience at times. Most people get more than enough of missionary or causal conversation. Feeling like we have been listened to and understood is not something we get every day.

Conversation puts individuals and their values in relation to topics, and each other. If individuals don't share their voice and seek common perspectives on a topic or interaction, other individuals will be happy to fill in what they think we need or deserve. One interaction or conversation may not change someone's mind when they disagree on an issue, but it starts the process of thinking along different lines of thought. As individuals recognize their position in their everyday relationships it can emphasize the personal control that they have to accept or reject from perspectives and labels. This recognition of control and influence over oneself can open an individual's eyes as to what it is they are communicating to others by their words and actions every day. It does seem ironic that many people will spend more time worrying about how they are dressed, or their hair, and almost no time on how they are communicating and being received by others. As we begin talking about the messages that we are sharing with each other it is an easy transition into the topic of culture and cultural exchange. Culture can be discussed as something that is variable, not specifically correct or incorrect, and even deriving from the circumstances of society. It is never fixed and as we are becoming part of a global culture we will see perspectives like this more readily making their way into everyday life.

This reframe can challenge the idea that being different is bad, wrong, something to be avoided, or even that the individual is somehow damaged or inferior. To articulate the problems and challenges that surround the issues of prejudice and intolerance there must first be an agreement that both opinions can equally coexist. The intolerance of one individual representing a static belief as an inflexible and unadoptable culture signals the disintegration of that culture. You have called this a monocultural perspective and many more people label this as plain ignorance. Since our conversations will center on a cultural perspective we can talk about the contrasting values, beliefs, and interpretations in a way that more respectfully circumvents the many personal defensive reactions. Personal attacks based on faulty logic or uneducated arguments will not have the same effect. It does create the opportunity for a person stating a belief to ask themselves if the sentiments that they utter are what they would like to have representing themselves personally and professionally. The challenge with any limiting set of beliefs is to get a manageable sandbox where all parties do not feel on the defensive and can respectfully share their position.

JOSEPH: You think your Kinkology, for lack of a better word, can serve society better than all the global philosophies before it?

Onex2: This is a funny question, because it seems to contrast what I am offering against all other information as if it were not born out of it. I am offering a personal philosophy based on respectful and democratic expression of ideas and discussion. I believe that the best way to change the world is to reflect on what we are doing and share our own personal journeys in it. The story is a vehicle of shared information and the listener has the choice as to what to accept or reject and nothing is forced upon them. When openly sharing information about very sensitive topics that include prejudice, injustice, discrimination, and everyday dramas, the vehicle that puts those things in context is our stories. If you've ever fallen in love with a character in a book or a movie you know that there are things that this character says or does that you don't agree with. I remember how my feelings towards a character got me through the boring parts of many books while getting me to think about topics I thought I had already made my mind up on. In the end, what was more important was that I was open to trying on the learnings for myself that were part of this character's development that I may have not done otherwise.

Though we might think of prejudice and discrimination as unfavorable, that is not always true. We are seeking to discriminate between immature and mature patterns of communication. We are seeking to discriminate those elements of our behavior that we could improve upon and it is not an easy process. I don't think I need to spell out that this is not the prejudice that I speak of when I say discrimination. When seeking to break through to an individual whose prejudice is long-standing I have often asked about the experience that they are having while attempting to hold onto prejudice and what that means to them. Our emotions are linked to preconceived perspectives on many topics. Every day we're all representing ideas about the world to ourselves, and sometimes the beliefs we adopt are limiting or unrealistic. In today's society prejudicial beliefs rob the victims as well as the victimizers of opportunities that can change their life.

JOSEPH: So what advice would you give people who seek to further this philosophy of social change and promote more intimate sharing amongst people?

Onex2: Science can tell us that the world is created and held together by atoms, but our minds recognize that each day our lives are connected together by stories. The stories we tell ourselves, and the stories that we share with each other can change the world. Every day each of us is challenged with the daunting task of introducing our ideas and vision to a world that passes that information around to shape communication and behavior along multiple channels to settle upon a shared future. I propose encouraging a scholar's perspective to combat intolerance through a combination of education and promoting the media and information that works with these topics that we care about. Asking if the information we are receiving and promoting is a primary source of information or a secondary source allows us to stop and look at the information itself. Inquiring about the strengths and weaknesses of information presented to us will allow us to discover if a story is slanted towards one way of thinking. This is something that is not always easy to do on first glance.

At this point we may begin to look for what isn't said, ignored, or even deleted from a statement or perspective. The books and movies that we suggest give us an opportunity to explore our world and ourselves while trying on themes/thoughts that we can use to make problems better. Discussing perspective from entertainment would better prepare us as individuals to ask about both sides of an argument in our personal interactions. The scholar's perspective means considering the information itself and how each person is a co-creator that will affirm or detract from an experience and its meaning for oneself and others.

Everyone in their life will come into some conflict with others as they live their lives. There will also be times that many of us will be called names or labeled in a way that we do not like or agree with. In learning about the scholar's perspective, we will be learning to respond instead of react when attempting to communicate respectfully with a person(s) that may engage in crude behavior. To me, if I were to think of a name or label that I have been called I will relate it in context with my entire life. In doing this I've found how meaningless any insult would be in labeling my overall goals and identity. The scholar's perspective can allow us to live as fully as possible and that includes looking at the perspectives we choose to live our lives with. This leaves the responsibility to seize opportunity and limitation of our abilities up to us. We all simply have to recognize it and create the meaning that we live our lives by every single day. Making an idealized monocultural decision for all of humanity dead, born, and unborn, a personal identity without acknowledgement or compromise for others will lead to unhealthy and maladaptive ways of thinking about ourselves, each other, and our world. By the way, notice I have stolen that monocultural label. That makes you a contributor to the scholar's perspective from this moment on.

JOSEPH: Thank you so much and I hope you will get a lot of good use out of it. Do you expect to utilize the "Scholar's Perspective" with those slaves who live within your household?

Onex2: Intelligence is something that I value and I want to know what it is they are thinking. I may choose my own direction but we all become stronger if we can learn from each other and then have a common direction that we all work towards together. As it applies to simple pleasure they will not be doing intellectual exercises that distract them from being sensual and a good slave. The time to brainstorm the best thing to do with your career is not when you're having sex. The scholar's perspective is an exercise in intellectual cultural leadership and decision making that can assist individuals in challenging the obstacles of their lives while improving their experience and, inevitably, their story. It encourages perspective-taking and can help to provide a logical foundation for questioning the status quo that we are all part of. Together we are inevitably building a more just society by recognizing what we are sharing and seeking to be that change it our world. These ideas are worth promoting through our networks so that we can be proud as writers and professionals, create characters, write articles, and teach students, so that others may be inspired to carry these ideas on. I will continue to create works that share these ideals. I will buy from people and purchase things that express these things that matter to me. I will advocate for others and live a life that shares these ideals with others so that they may be carried across the globe. I will recommend works that belong to this perspective so that people across the globe may be able to suggest and carry on this trend. Many of these things we will all do anyway. Doing them consciously allows us to design in elements that can be incorporated by others so that they will be more widely communicated and understood. I want to recommend that individuals look up the term "frown power". Stetson Kennedy came up with this very effective social signal to signal others that what they were doing was not okay.

JOSEPH: Are you aware that you have connected your sexuality to every part of your life?

Onex2: Are you aware that you haven't realized that your sexuality is connected to every part of your life?

JOSEPH: Hmmm. I really have never thought that deeply into it before.

Onex2: All of us are focused to different degrees on the various elements of our psyche and biology. For some their sexuality is something that is the most important thing and there are other people for whom it isn't a big deal. You probably fall into that "not a big deal" area. That doesn't mean it couldn't become one if someone made you defensive about your sexual identity or you suddenly became curious about a thought, person, desire, or act, which led you down that road. Do you agree?

JOSEPH: I do. I am going to skip back just a bit and connect this point to what we are talking about. Are you proposing that dialogue about these themes and identities can be worked through by posting comments discussing them through Amazon on products itself? That way people will begin to consider these questions as they watch movies or grab books?

Onex2: Yes. I am an activist and an advocate for these issues by getting people to share how what they are reading, writing, watching, and thinking about relates to different themes and concepts. Connect them to groups and email. Give people search terms and encourage them to think outside of the box. Being an activist and an advocate means that awareness must be raised and I should be garnishing support from others as I go. This is not a lone cause and I want to share the idea with others in this way. Notice I keep using the word "share". On these topics we all have something to offer and I don't want indoctrination so that everyone believes it is all one way. I want to instill cooperation and collaboration so that people recognize that they have a voice in what is happening and they have a responsibility to themselves and others to not be part of the problem. That means understanding what each of us is responsible for and encouraging others to think about ideas and supporting the choices they make. Attempting to control other people's actions and interpretations when they don't agree with our own is wrong. It is a thought crime that ends with people suffering.

Attempting to control and create the perfect image of married life has ended in more divorce. Attempting to control people's sexual knowledge of safe sex has ended in more teens becoming pregnant. Attempting to control religious interpretation of scripture has led to more religious institutions and people feeling disconnected and divorced from the faith that they once knew. I can go on and on. What we all have to begin with is the idea that how we relate to others and ourselves creates and sustains the environments that we live in. Anyone can treat something that they don't know about or connect with as different from what is familiar to them and preferred. To create a better world, we must start with how we are communicating with each other. That means sharing what matters to us on public reviews of products and services, because people will see it and read it. That means hints and outright statements on social media. That means going out to the State House and supporting marriage equality for all people. That means fighting for free speech even when we don't like what is being said. That means practicing what we preach and not thinking twice about asking people that are authority figures why they did something. That means challenging people who create barriers to change and treat one group of people this way and another group another way. That means taking care of each other and creating partnerships with people who are part of these systems and communicating what we expect of them and the work they are doing. So at the end of the day you can get the questions you have answered and not feel ashamed or awkward that you have this question.

When people are ordering movies or looking up info on a movie, something about that movie has an appeal to them that they wish to experience. Movies are written to portray a slice of a person, or people's lives with a set of particular characteristics. They are designed to appeal to specific demographics while attempting to keep some elements as universal as possible. The people who will read this work are part of a community that is a demographic, and represents a slice of the population curious and interested in certain phenomena that I hope I am connecting to as universally thematic. These repeating themes are culturally specific indicators that often come back to similar questions and connect out again to the lives and worlds of imagination and spirit. They play a part in how the next generation will re-imagine the world and I want everyone to be able to see examples of themselves in the media. Then we can talk about healthy and unhealthy ideas. We can talk about what it means to live a certain way or plan to be a specific occupation. The difference here is the power of what we should do or be must rest with the people and not with the misguided judgments of what is right or wrong for everyone. Laws are needed and laws have been changed because they have been outdated, but how we live our life and the meanings we ascribe to what we do should be adaptable by us. We should recognize we have the power to live and seek, not to impose on others or their freedoms in doing so. I am against anyone who thinks that they have the social authority to create a rule that says because a person loves the same sex or loves more than one person, or because they ascribe roles in their love making, that they are somehow less worthy or valid with their love. I think once we get passed these issues a lot of the problems in the world will be better.

Hearing from Eli

JOSEPH: Do you mind if I ask Eli some of these questions?

Onex2: Not at all. She is at work right now and will be happy for the distraction. Let me pull up a chat window.

(I watch him start up his PC and sign on to chat. He gets in touch with Eli and he types quickly. "I am with a friend and he would like to ask you some questions. Here is his name on gchat its balanceheart, IM him and answer everything 100% and honestly.)

Onex2: She should be in contact in a moment.

(We both hear my cell phone beep with the IM message.)

Eli: Hello. I was asked to contact you.

JOSEPH: Hi. Would you mind answering some questions for me?

Eli: I would be happy to. What would you like to know?

JOSEPH: How would you define slavery?

Eli: In the past it had the singular meaning of being the unwilling bondage of another person. Today slavery in many forms still exists but lifestyle slavery is something that is different and consensual. In terms of our relationship I would probably say service and loyalty to another person in return for safety and control.

JOSEPH: How would you describe your relationship?

Eli: In many ways a partnership built on mutual respect and love. I give myself to him and he takes me. We push each other to become better people, to learn, and to grow.

JOSEPH: Do you consider yourself to be a slave?

Eli: I identify with that term, yes. More than sub or servant or the like.

JOSEPH: Can you say more about how you identify?

Eli: In general or in terms of slave?

JOSEPH: Is there a difference?

Eli: I identify as a lot of things. One question is vague while the other is specific. I'm really not sure what you're asking for.

JOSEPH: What are the most important elements when you think of who you are? Describe yourself as you would want someone to know you intimately.

Eli: I would want someone to know that I am hardworking and dedicated to my goals and dreams. I would want them to know that I am completely in love with my partner who is also my master. I identify as Jewish, polyamorous, and pansexual, open-minded, and that I am confident and comfortable with who I am.

JOSEPH: Have you met any discrimination to who you are or who you present yourself to be?

Eli: I have come across some overt discrimination based on my "out and proud" presentation of my sexual identity. As for my M/s relationship, my polyamorous relationships, and my BDSM preferences, not yet. I keep those private because I expect bias and discrimination and do not feel supported by the community enough to defend myself and my beliefs. In many ways it is easier to pretend to be "normal".

JOSEPH: If you found someone who was curious about the lifestyle would you take them by the hand even when you feel a bit uneasy?

Eli: Do you mean talk about the lifestyle and answer questions? Or enter a relationship with them?

JOSEPH: Talk about it and maybe bring them into your relationship?

Eli: I am always delighted to talk and answer questions about my lifestyle because it means someone was open-minded enough to be curious. As for bringing them into my relationship, that would depend on who they were and the circumstances of our relationship. If they were a Dom I would direct them to my master. If they were a sub, I might teach by sharing with them as a friend, but not in a romantic relationship. If we are talking about bringing someone into my current established relationship, that would depend upon my master. I would not be leading, he would.

JOSEPH: How would you go about adding someone to the relationship that you thought would be a good fit?

Eli: I am not sure. I would likely befriend them and introduce them to my master. If becoming friends wasn't possible due to distance or scheduling, I would probably try to set up dates for the three of us. I don't have much confidence in this area and would be more comfortable letting my master take the lead here.

JOSEPH: Have you always been interested in being a slave?

Eli: I have always been interested in a D/S relationship; becoming a slave was just a more permanent form of that relationship.

JOSEPH: Have the experiences you have had in this role impacted your life outside of the relationship you have with your master?

Eli: Absolutely. My master has a huge impact on my self-image, self-esteem, and confidence. He has pushed me to become better at many things, in the relationship and outside of it. Through his guidance my relationships with others have improved and my ability to withstand stress and pressure has gotten better. I am a much more confident and secure woman now than I was two years ago. A little confidence goes a long way in improving life inside and outside a relationship.

JOSEPH: Can you give an example or two of how it has helped?

Eli: I am in the process of applying to law school. Confidence and stability present well in interviews and without the security and stability of my private life I would not be able to juggle the workload and pressure I do now.

JOSEPH: How do you imagine the future?

Eli: That is very vague, but I can work with it… I expect I will go to law school, hopefully somewhere nearby while he develops his career. Other than that, not much is certain. In the long term though, I expect to stay with him for the rest of my life. If you would like something more specific you will need a more specific question.

JOSEPH: How about others that he will want in the picture and in the house?

Eli: I want that too. I would feel balanced to have another person to love who loves both me and him as well. There are parts of our relationship that would benefit from another person. With three or more people in one relationship it becomes more work to keep everyone happy and satisfied but I think we can do it and that it would be worth the effort.

JOSEPH: Is there a number of people that is too many for your relationship that he may bring in? Would you leave over a problem or conflict in this area?

Eli: If I left over a conflict in this area then that number of people was too many. I cannot say what number would be the limit but I know it would be reached when we can no longer juggle the needs and responsibility of such a large household. The number of people would go up of course if everyone is mature and on-board with making the relationship work. Even in a two-person relationship, one person with too much baggage or not enough maturity can sabotage the relationship.

JOSEPH: How did you figure out you were polyamorous or poly?

Eli: When I was 11 and dreaming about getting married I would dream of having a husband and wife. It is how I've been wired from the very beginning.

JOSEPH: Is it hard to find people who want the same thing?

Eli: It is rare, but not difficult. The internet makes it easy to build communities.

JOSEPH: What did you imagine life would be like at age 11 in a poly relationship?

Eli: Haha! Something dreamy where everyone loved each other. Where I could go adventuring and the people I love wouldn't be lonely because they had each other. I was big on adventuring when I was 11.

JOSEPH: That is sweet. What are the experiences that have defined you in your mind as a slave?

Eli: I think what defines me most as a slave is entrusting my master with control. It is very internal and not a light matter for me. Every time I submit willingly I am showing him I trust him completely and he shows me his love through his care of that trust.

JOSEPH: It is more than just sex for both of you then? How do you know this for yourself?

Eli: Of course it is more than just sex. I see this every day when he smiles at me in the morning. It shows in the care he has taken to build me into a beautiful person. Someone interested in only sex would not need to take that time. I feel very confident the relationship we have means more than just sex. Although sexual pleasure is a large part of our relationship, it is not everything

JOSEPH: What has been the best sexual adventures or experiences you have had in this role?

Eli: The first time I experienced sub-space, the first time I passed out from pleasure, and the many times after. Sub-space is like passing out without the tension and buzzing. It feels peaceful, like afterglow combined with white fluffiness. The first time it happened to me was in the middle of sex and I had heard of it before but I didn't realize that is what was happening. I tried to tell my master what was going on but he just smiled into my face and drove harder. Afterwards I always feel more submissive, like I can give my master more. I feel happy. Sometimes I pass out during sex. I don't always remember afterwards but it comes with overwhelming sensation, before and after. Passing out is more like a black-out sensation. I get short of breath and loose connection to everything except what is happening right then. Usually I have cum many times that night already, but sometimes it comes quickly. I am not sure what causes it one time as opposed to another, perhaps my breathing, perhaps something else. I remember my master laughed at me the first time I asked him what happened. "You passed out", he said and I didn't believe him. I believe him now because he's shown me again and again.

JOSEPH: Is that what you understand your sub-space to be?

Eli: No. That is blacking out. The first description was of sub-space. Sub-space is white and glowy. Blacking out is dark and breathless.

JOSEPH: How important is it for you to get into your sub-space? Does it have the same intensity of achievement as your orgasm?

Eli: I love my sub-space for the emotions it brings, but it is not necessary for submission or pleasure. It actually lowers the intensity of the orgasms during, but sometimes lower intensity is good. It makes me feel safe and protected, even if what is happening to me is on the painful end. Perhaps especially then.

JOSEPH: Sounds like you were gifted with a good ability to orgasm. Is your orgasm itself part of how you play in your role?

Eli: It is. When my master asks for it I can give him even my orgasm.

JOSEPH: What do you mean you give it to him?

Eli: When he tells me to orgasm my body responds. It is part of my submission, giving him control over everything.

JOSEPH: Is it possible to partake in degradation or humiliation activities and maintain respect for the person or people involved?

Eli: The best degradation or humiliation is done by someone who respects you enough to know your mind and what you feel and think. Besides, the contrast of respecting someone against the utter intensity of the emotion is what can make it delicious. At least for me.

JOSEPH: Sounds like you have discovered a lot of things about yourself in this role. Can you tell me a story or two about a boundary that was pushed and you ended up being surprised or something you didn't even know you liked until it happened?

Eli: The first thing that comes to mind is something seemingly small. Outside of my relationship I have taken martial arts and when someone smacks or touches my face I have a strong and instantaneous reaction. The first time my master smacked my face during sex I was almost surprised out of my orgasm, but my body responded so positively that I was swept back in. It has now become one of my favorite things to ramp up an orgasm. I appreciate being pushed; I do not want the boundaries I have. The path my Master has led me on has been full of discovery. It hasn't always been easy for me and I don't always go mentally willing, but I appreciate where it has brought me and urge my master never to give up on me. I love the journey and where it has brought us. I have to go people are walking in.

JOSEPH: Thanks for answering my questions. I hope we can talk again.

Eli: I would enjoy that. Bye.

(I look up from the computer and close the lid.)

Onex2: How was your chat?

JOSEPH: It was nice. Eli seems very intelligent and it shows that she has a strong will of her own.

Onex2: This isn't the 1950's where she would be expected to be chained to the stove and not have to worry about money. Eli has dreams about a career and wants to take care of her family. Both of us will have debt when we are done with school and the combined debt will amount to the price of a mansion in itself. My grandfather used to be able to work through the summer and have enough money to go to college for a year, eat well, buy books, and live on campus. Society is not structured in the same way it was ten years ago, so I shouldn't complain about this change about sixty years later. All of us should understand what economic injustice is and start to recognize that too many systems have been set up to nickel and dime people into poverty. A correct argument must also be made that someone must pay for this standard of living and the poor and the middle class certainly do.

JOSEPH: Would you say that economic injustice is something that plays a big part in how you live?

Onex2: It plays a big part in how all of us live. We will never be able to know for sure how big a part. It didn't cause me to be kinky, but it has made me realized that I can be kinky and create a kinky family unit that can take care of more than just me. Money is something that is getting harder and harder to hold onto, and that is worse if you live alone or you're the only bread winner. I believe that it is this struggle to make a buck that will cause people to come together as different types of relationships form and take on the stereotypes and bias that created the system. I don't need the approval of an institution to tell me how I live is good. I don't like that I have to work over 40 hours a week just to begin to meet the bills and get ahead. I hate that the future seems to be forecasting more of the same and getting worse. That is of course depending on who you are listening to. Right now we can listen to Republicans talk about how things can't be getting better under Obama, and if we only taxed people other than the 1% we could fix the country. There are so many lies being thrown around I wonder how anyone believes anything. It is nice to see John Stewart and Colbert Report use the same tactics that both Democrats and Republicans use to reframe something as better than it is. I will be content when the meek find a good master and the kinky inherit the Earth. We are going to spur a wave of change that begins at home and I hope that people will seek me out and tell me about it.

THE END FOR NOW…

Want to share epic tale with the world?

Got a story to tell that you believe the world has to know. Pitch your story here by emailing JosephS@Santiago-inc.com or balanceheart@hotmail.com

- You must be 18 years or older and be able to prove that.

- You must own the rights and have permission to use all materials submitted to us.

- You must have a good story that will hold our interest and entertain others.

- Want to know more? Share your story and leave your mark!

www.ingramcontent.com/pod-product-compliance
Lightning Source LLC
Chambersburg PA
CBHW031521270326
41930CB00006B/472